Table of Contents

Welcome to Rad Dad #19

This issue is conflicted…I say that with a mix of disappointment and pride. Usually, I let the issues create themselves, sometimes asking specific people to write for it, and otherwise collecting what people send in to me. Yes, that normally means scrambling to finish the zine a few days before it goes to the printer. However, I had big plans for this issue. Like the last one—which had a theme—I wanted to make all the essays work around a particular subject: how we talk to kids about difficult issues such as racism, sexism, environmental crisis, and so on. In retrospect, it seems that I was preparing for a tough winter to come. For my family, there was violence in our neighborhood as a number of young men were killed, friends of ours were assaulted in their homes, domestic violence happened in a family we were close to. Suddenly, it seemed I was just trying to keep up with things—let alone talk about them with my kids. But they were listening; they were witnesses to it all and witnesses to how we, the adults in their lives, reacted. Then there were the social issues that kept happening: bullying and suicide, the Oscar Grant verdict, the election.

Despite all this, this issue came together quickly, people volunteered essays, people wrote about pain and difficulty but also about the beauty of parenthood, about love and learning and letting go.

So in some ways this issue has conflicting tones and experiences but as I think about it, we as parents do as well. Welcome to Rad Dad #19!

And as always I invite you send in stories, interviews, drawings, for the next issue…because Rad Dad is all about you!

Tomas Moniz

Doing Something is Better Than Nothing

by Tomas Moniz

Parenting has taught me a lot about dealing with things I'd rather not deal with. I've been forced to breathe deeply and make the call to the doctor at three in the morning: "um, my daughter won't stop crying," and when the doctor asks why she's crying, I've had to confess, "Well, I kinda dropped her today."

That never feels good to admit.

Or I've had to clench my mouth shut tightly and just let my daughter have her feelings, be disappointed, resist the urge to placate her, to try to "make" her feel better by saying something inane like, "well your little ten year old friend is a dick."

Definitely, not good parental role modeling. I've learned to deal with larger, seemingly inhuman bureaucracies such as the school system—with its rules and policies that punish children for their parents' choice or responsibilities. No, I don't think it's fair that my seventh grader gets an F in classes because I took her on a trip to see a sick relative. I've learned to face a police and justice system that views children as criminals first and people second.

Parenting has shown me that both the little things and big things in life can be sometimes daunting to face. As the saying goes, shit ain't easy. Life is messy. People—messy. Friendship is work and commitment as well as fun and pleasurable. Just like parenting.

Sometimes I wish I could ignore things, overlook stuff I don't want to face; pretend I didn't know—just go on with my everyday routine.

Parenting, however, has demonstrated that there are the choices we need to make between letting some things slide while focusing on others.

My daughter arriving home ten minutes late from school might be ok now and then. I can raise an eyebrow and shrug off her, "what, the bus was late!," exasperated remark when I ask why she's not on time. Because when she's out at night and forgets to call when I explicitly explained that I expected her to, that ain't something you can let slide. It's something you have to address, and it's difficult to hold her to the agreed upon consequences. It's painful to hear her anger, her frustration—to be the target of her unmitigated teenage rage. And that shit's scary.

So parenting has taught me how to stand firm but that some things are negotiable—there's a balance between holding your child accountable and creating transparency in your agreements.

Let me stop stalling.

A friend of mine was arrested for domestic violence. There's a story there. There are reasons for his anger and even empathy around the whole situation: towards him, towards his partner. The whole affair is sad. It's painful. In the end, perhaps it will all be for the best for both of them and their kids.

But there is no excuse for violence in a relationship. None. Ever.

The crisis is over. She moved out of their home. They have a routine set up. Things are almost back to normal. People in my circle of friends are even joking about it.

And that is what bothers me, what makes me uncomfortable.

I started to ask around: what is my role? How do I address this with my daughters? How to be a true friend?

I don't want to be the one to constantly bring it up every time I see him, but I also don't want a "business as usual" type of friendship or a "don't ask, don't tell" relationship even though that is so much easier: if I don't know about it, I guess I don't have to make any tough choices. I remember when the Chris Brown and Rhianna incident occurred. I immediately talked to my kids about it, especially my youngest daughter who was very into both of them. I asked how they felt about hearing the news. I didn't want to let this opportunity slip: a chance to address the unacceptability of domestic violence, to establish a clear "zero-tolerance" policy. Some things can slide; physical and emotional abuse can't.

Chris Brown was ostracized; we as a family severed ties with him and his music. And the cool thing is most of the population did as well. His musical career seems to be over.

But what to do with my friend?

Soon after all this happened, I spoke with another friend of mine—a woman—a person who had been in an abusive relationship in the past, and she gave me some advice I hold dearly now. She said when she was going through it, that she wished people would have done something, anything. She looked at me and stated, "sometimes doing the wrong thing is better than doing nothing."

I understood immediately why I was so uncomfortable—I could see how easy doing nothing could have been. Denial is powerful. But as parenting has taught me some things can't slide and so sometimes you just gotta grin and bear it. You have to face it.

I want to thank my kids for making me learn this lesson.

I knew I needed to talk to him before he moved off the block, so one night when he came over to borrow something, I did.

We stood out on my stoop, and we talked. First I expressed my anger and disappointment. Then I expressed my dilemma. I told him I knew it would be work, but that I wanted to be the kind of friend who is willing to both stand up for someone and hold them accountable. I expressed my concerns about how he was taking responsibility for his actions.

I did acknowledge that I had no answers; only questions. But I told him I'm willing to struggle to find those answers with him, together.
We hugged, and he left.

A few days later, I planned to bring up the subject again with my daughters and twenty-year-old son, who was visiting. We had talked about it here and there, and they have heard me, their mother, and other friends talking about the incident; arguing over it; gossiping about it. My youngest daughter and I saw the cop cars in front of their house when it happened and I said to her almost in jest, "I hope that's not what I think it is." I cringe, thinking about how uncritical a statement that is in regards to domestic abuse. I feel like I should apologize to her over my seeming ambivalence.

So we were all sitting around the table, my two daughters and my son, eating dinner. I was feeling nervous, somehow incompetent, like I should have something specific to say, some clear concise message to tell them. I don't know what to say. I just wanted to be honest with them.

Finally, I confessed, "I am angry that I don't know what to do or say. I feel like a hypocrite singing that song about Chris Brown needing to get his ass kicked after what he did, and yet when it happens on my street I'm at a loss as to what I should do. Just because I'm a friend with someone doesn't mean they're not accountable."

"You know it's not your fault dad," says my youngest, like I'm acting foolish.

Getting chastised by your kids is another thing you learn to deal with from parenting.
"I know," I said, "I just don't want to sweep this under the rug. Domestic violence whether it's emotional or physical is never ok. No matter what."

I was looking at my two daughters like I'm telling them that they should never stand for it, when I realized my son was sitting right there. Looking at me. I looked at him.

I realized I haven't had a conversation like this in a while, talking about sex education was one thing, talking domestic violence another.
My son shook his head up and down slowly. "I know dad," he said I know, and he looked me in the eye, "that shit is totally fucked up."

And he meant it.

It was one of the most reassuring moments in my life. I realized what had also been bothering me was talking with my son about it. It's strange to love this young person so much, and for years feeling like I could control his actions. Now he stands taller than me, muscular, lean, a man, and I have no control over anything anymore in his life—except for kicking in money for his rent—and yet I still have such expectations of him. And he may let me down in the future or make mistakes in relationships, but one thing I think he knows is that domestic abuse is a line you don't cross.

Hearing him say that with such conviction, without equivocation in front of his sisters was a profound moment for me.

"Thank you," I said.

And we all went on to other things.

As the weeks pass, I bring it up with my daughters now and then. My middle child has a boyfriend. And I see how quickly I will have no control in her life too. It's hard to let go. But I'm gonna do it. With love and with encouragement and with trust.

They taught me that.

This issue of Rad Dad is dedicated to all those who are victims of violence: at the hands of the police, of bullies, of their own family.

I promise you I will never look the other way.

I promise you I will do something whether it's the right thing or not at the time.

I promise. I will.

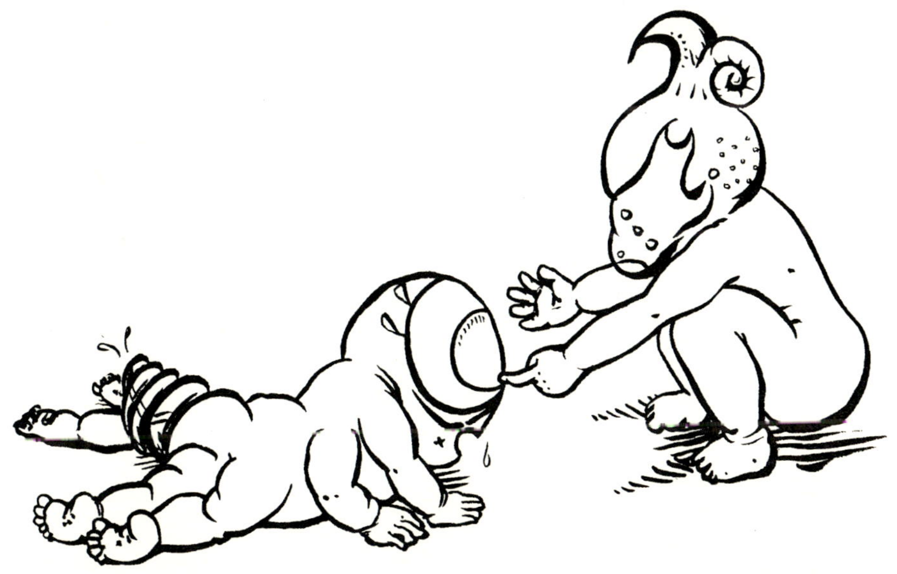

Responses about Domestic Abuse from Folks on the Anarchist Parenting Listserv

I posted the following question to the Anarchist Parenting Listserv and these were a couple of the responses I received which really helped me think about a plan of action. These are emails, not essays, so there is some anger and emotion, and I really needed to hear it. I thank you.

Initial email:
Warning: this may be a trigger for some people; it is about domestic abuse.

Hello, I'm Tomas Moniz, editor of Rad Dad, and I have a problem that I'm hoping people might have some suggestions for or know of places to look.
Long story short: a friend of mine was arrested for domestic abuse and supposedly there has been a history of "minor" abuse on both sides over the years...He was arrested, they've separated, and things seem back to business as usual...people in my life are even saying they understand why it happened like it is an understandable thing?

So now I'm left with the "so what to do?" I don't know what my responsibility is in all of this...I've had talks with my kids about it because they all know we were talking about it and now it seems no one is and that it's out of sight, out of mind. I feel slightly hypocritical because my kids love music and when Chris Brown hit Rhianna we talked about it and decided to no longer support Chris Brown. We made a clear decision...but when my neighbor and friend does it...it's like nothing happened, there's a silence around it.

Somehow I just feel the business as usual approach is avoiding the work that needs to be done?

I guess I'm wondering what people think about this...is there a support zine for men who have been abusive and for male allies on how to hold people accountable and how to be a supportive friend, I'm not sure if there is something I should be doing as a friend of his, Thanks... Tomas

Response One:
Hey there—the first responsibility is: FIGHT THE FUCKING PATRIARCHY/ KYRIARCHY!!! {It is} all dudes responsibility, always, all the time, with everyone. But for something a little more...
I don't know of a zine or resource on accountability other than The Revolution Starts at Home. While unfortunate that there isn't lots out there, TRSAH—a book that you can print out or download from online—is fucking amazing.

Things start with talking about the idea of mutual abuse and the myths around domestic violence in general. Mutual abuse—the idea that two partners in a relationship abuse each other "mutually" or "equally" is generally a crock of shit. It sounds like Tomas ain't buying it right now which is awesome. It actually helps enable abuse. Abuse isn't a single incident or a series of incidents, but establishing systems and patterns of power within a relationship. 99% of the time in hetero-relationships this falls along gender lines with men assuming control in the relationship. Things that are often tagged as mutual abuse are:

- survivors responding to the abuse violently or aggressively in the moment
- pre-empting abusers in self-defense
- "emotional abuse" (to which the abuser says "I wouldn't have hit her but she pushed me to my limit with her words. I didn't know what else to do")

Reactions to abuse:

Often, the idea of mutual abuse is put out by abusers or their supporters in a means to justify their behavior. The truth is, "mutual abuse" can only happen if it isn't "abuse" but a series of isolated incidents.

When specific situation arises, I would place Tomas' greatest responsibility, beyond doing what he can to support the family through a difficult time, to focus on supporting the mother as she goes towards safer space physically and emotionally. This doesn't necessarily mean being a therapist, but helping her access resources relevant to the situation—domestic violence centers; support groups; therapists; etc.—maybe watching the kids while she goes somewhere or rides to and from an appointment if she needs one.

In regards to the abusive partner, it gets a little more complicated. First, the best action towards accountability would come with the approval of the survivor. If no one is checking with the survivor on how they want the community to respond to the abuse, someone should. That's really important.

I would suggest thinking about how to use this situation as a means to educate about the realities of domestic violence. If people are saying that they understand why it happened, that's a perfect time to talk about it. Or just handing out zines to folk about the topic.

Some really good ones are:
•UBUNTU's Supporting Survivors of Sexual Assault
•Our Own Response: The Revolution Starts at Home

The most important place to start is making sure that the abuser doesn't think that Tomas is going to give them a pass on this, but still expects them to be friends or whatever the relationship was before.

Isolating abusers from communities just sends them onto other ones.

It can be as simple as encouraging them to see a counselor or therapist, and when, if they say yes, holding them to it.

It can be as big as telling them that you're willing to sit with them every night and talk about abuse, and starting a men's group that talks about patriarchy/kyriarchy and working on their shit together and spreading the work as wide as they can.

Or anything in between.

Other resources are:
•The NorthWest Network- nwnetwork.org
CARA (Communities Against Rape and Abuse) - cara-seattle.org
•Incite: Women of Color Against Violence-incite-national.org
•Generation 5 www.generationfive.org (relevant to parents as it deals with child sexual abuse)

Response Two:

Ugh. I grew up in a community with a lot of domestic violence and no one ever intervened or ever said it was not ok. It was always framed as mutual combat, even though it was only ever the women walking around with a black eye or hunks of hair pulled out of their head. Or it was excused because the dudes were often drunk when it happened. (Why does that make it better??)

How much of a friend is this person? Enough to have real talk? Could you say, "hey, that upset me and I don't think it was alright, are you getting any kind of support to make sure you don't do anything like that again?"

Along with the conspiracy of silence there's also a shunning that happens; perps are shunned but shunning doesn't amount to holding someone accountable. And by just shunning the abuser, we avoid having real conversations about how it happens, how someone ends up doing something like that, and how to deal with it, avoid it, change it. And so other people who may have a tendency in that direction aren't going to look for help because of the shunning.

I don't know, man, we're really not very good at this stuff. I do think that the nature of your relationship with the people involved should be the starting point for figuring out what you do.

To My Brothers in the Movement from David Gilbert

This open letter is a call, made both passionately and emphatically, for movement men to get fully involved in childcare. Childcare is one of the most demanding yet rewarding jobs in the world and is essential to advancing the struggle. I've been surprised to learn that in this day and age that responsibility still falls overwhelmingly on women. Men's failure in this regard is not only unfair but also hurts our movement since it is a major impediment to women's participation, to the full range of contribution they can make. But even more, if truth be told, this aloofness damages men the most because we cut ourselves off from the regular interactions that can enrich our lives in many ways. Children ask the questions that make us think more deeply about everything, exude the energy that buoys our spirits, embody the potential that gives us hope for the future. It's for the children that we fight to make a better world. Brothers, it is way past due to get fully involved in childcare. David Gilbert (anti-imperialist political prisoner)

Letter to My 67 Kids

by David Cahn

Writer's Note: I am a childcare worker at small non-profit center in downtown Seattle. I am a "floater" in the mornings, meaning I cover co-worker's breaks and vacations in any rooms needed, and am the pre-K teacher for the afternoon. That means that most weeks I am taking care of children anywhere between 3 months and 5 years old. After a little more than three years I feel like I have hit my stride and know how to effectively care for and educate a room full of young children. It took a lot of trial and error and frustration but I can say with more confidence than most that childcare is not a job that one is "naturally" suited for. It takes a lot experience and specific skills that need to be continually learned and refined.

I definitely did not plan on working long term at this center. I thought I would work here until I could land a job at some non-profit, hopefully being some professional organizer of some type. No longer wanting to work at a non-profit, working in childcare has had a profound impact on me and my politics.

The intersection between radical/left politics, children, childcare, parenting and intergenerational movement building is endlessly fascinating to me. Seeing Rad Dad accepting submissions on talking to children about difficult issues inspired the letter below.

P.S. I recognize childcare as a necessary resource for working and middle class families and obviously families that use childcare are not all "bad" and "exploitative." My center happens to serve the rich, while my co-workers and I struggle from paycheck to paycheck and it is from this situation my writing is based!

Hi there!

I take care of you—change your diapers, help you go potty, feed you, read to you, hug you, lead you in activities and games, talk with you, chase and tickle you, and try to help you become a decent human being—for 40 hours a week. Of course I do not do this by myself, I work with almost 30 other people. While your parents work at law firms, city government, Fortune 500 companies, and fancy high tech corporations—you're brought up in and by a community that mainly consists of Filipina and Chinese immigrants, Thai and Laotian refugees, and working class Black and white women. Most of us have been gentrified out of the city limits.

I'm sorry. I'm sorry for the times—all too many—that I have lost my temper with you, yelled at you and behaved irresponsibly. I am sorry for the structure of our center that segregates you by age and the daily routines that regiment your time. My day is hard and tiring but I recognize that your days are just the same. I'm sorry for the times you are just tired and over-stimulated, and want to have some quiet time or to be comforted. I try my best to give you that when needed, but there are plenty other instances where I have ignored your obvious needs and just forced you to get ready for the next part of our day. I am sorry for this too.

I am so sorry that we have given in to the demands of vocal parents and pushed this bizarre idea of "kindergarten readiness" on you. I am sorry for the countless times I've had you sit down at a table and practice tracing your name or glue construction paper patterns together. I don't know exactly what a liberating childcare center would look like, but I know it would focus 100% on letting you play, work and learn together in how to treat each other decently. We do that currently—in spite of our center's focus.

We have fun together though, don't we? It's a daily lesson for me to see you live fully in each moment and enjoy yourself by any means necessary. Even if your teachers are running around frantically trying to get our breaks done or find enough staffing to take you on a field trip, you are making sure you are having fun, playing and enjoying life. When my shift is feeling long or hard, I am inspired by you to lighten up, be silly and inject a little play into my life. Adults get so used to work and adult responsibilities that we begin to place inhibitions and rules on our behavior, as any boss could hope to. We could do well to learn from your example!

At story time at the public library, you are always the best behaved kids. The children of upper class helicopter parents and the working class kids of other local daycares are invariably the ones who are louder, busier and not minding their caretakers. For the most part you all sit there quietly and politely, genuinely interested in the stories and enthusiastically participating in the activities. I'm ambivalent about this. Part of me is very proud of your behavior, but I also can't help but think we are complicit in disciplining your bodies and hearts for a lifetime of work under capitalism. We've trained you well to sit still and pay attention to the adult/authority figure in front of the room. In one sense this will serve you very well as you grow older, but it does make me a little sad to think about what we are setting you up for. It is also sobering to think that this disciplining and socializing is actually part of what your parents pay for and expect from our center.

Childcare is harder work, both physically and emotionally, than people who have not done it can really know. At the same time, it is a joy to be a part of your lives. To watch you grow up and just be your awesome little people selves is so great and amazing to witness. It makes me angry sometimes that this is used as partial justification for our low pay and low status. From your parents and others we get messages like: "I couldn't do what you do." "Thanks for helping raise my kid, here are some donuts." "You are all great. You obviously aren't in this line of work for the money."

Why can't or shouldn't we be in this line of work for the money? Just because I can take some happiness out of my work and my relationships with you, your smiles, unfortunately, do not buy me anything. Furthermore, your mom and dad could not "have it all"—successful careers and a family, without us. Many of them—very successful lawyers, business people and techies—are or have been absolutely at a loss for how to raise you as babies and young children and constantly ask for us for guidance and advice. It's a shame that it needs to be constantly stated, as this system can't seem to grasp this idea, but you all are very important as the next generation. What else matters in life than what we pass on to you?

Capitalist logic says our work is "women's work," and nothing of real value. Childcare workers—both paid and unpaid—then get the true social cost and need of your care taken out of our paychecks, backsides and lives. Your parents come to our center individually, and pay their expensive tuition individually. I wonder if any of them have the sense of the small community me and your other teachers have created around you. Regardless of what rooms we work in, we all consider you "our kids," and love each of you.

I find it fascinating that you won't remember any of us as you grow older. Some of you as babies, would cry inconsolably every time your primary caretaker walked out of the room for her 15 minute or lunch break. I wonder what of our relationships and interactions you will take forward in your life. I imagine most of you will remain in the class position of your parents, having others work for and under you and have others serve your needs. I wish it was possible for you to remember that it was mostly working class women of color and immigrants who brought you up and prepared you for the rest of your life. It was from this circle of women and a few men, such as myself, that you had your needs met and laid the foundations for your social skill and sense of self. As you have children of your own, please remember that many of my coworkers and your caretakers are mothers and grandmothers themselves, who gave so much of their time, love, energy and patience to your development—and found ways to save some for their own children.

I like to think that this will magically guarantee

you to side with the working class, people of color and immigrants as you grow older. But I have no illusions of that happening in a country where countless white people were and are raised by women slaves, domestic workers and nannies of color—and then go on to maintain this racist system. A moral balance does exist though, and it will be on you to pay back later, whether you know it or not.

Of course we are not your parents or biological family, but I do believe that on a day-to-day basis you do not accept the capitalist divisions between your parents and us—your caretakers. We are all adults trying our best to raise and prepare you for a life to be well-lived. I hope you won't grow to accept these real and material divisions that exist as "natural" or "normal." I hope you will do what you can to build a true and caring community around you and not let capitalism continue to estrange us from ourselves, our work and each other.

Thanks for letting me be a small part of your life.

David

David Cahn is a childcare worker in downtown Seattle. His blog, Paid in Smiles, can be found at childcareworkers.wordpress.com. He is also an organizer with the Seattle Solidarity Network (www.seasol.net).

Interview with Jeff Conant

by Tomas Moniz

Editor's note: As I've said before, one of the goals I had when I started Rad Dad was to get to know other fathers, to share stories, to talk politics and fears and surprises we experienced as we became gathers. The stories are always fascinating and inspiring, sometimes painful, sometimes cautionary. But always the stories are reminders of how the best asset we can have as fathers is to be reflective—to remember fathering is a process and not a simple thing. Here are two interviews. Enjoy!

Can you tell us about some of the projects you have been a part of over the last few years?

Aside from raising a daughter and trying to earn a living? I recently published my book A Poetics of Resistance, about the Zapatista movement. Much of that was researched and written over a decade ago when I lived in Chiapas. I also published in 2008 a book that took eight years to complete, called A Community Guide to Environmental Health—a grassroots educational manual on everything from compost toilets to toxic waste. That book involved travel to communities around the world struggling to address environmental degradation and the livelihood costs associated with it. It's from the base of that work that I now find myself doing media work with a number of climate justice organizations, essentially trying to get the word out about solutions to the ecological crisis that are both just and ecological, as opposed to market-driven.

I'm developing popular education materials on human rights issues, doing some freelance journalism, trying to make time for some fiction and creative non-fiction projects I've had going for too many years now, playing with puzzles and Play-doh, and going to the zoo.

Was it a specific choice to become a parent?

It was, but not an easy one. I had always been ambivalent about children—both having them and being around them—undoubtedly because my own family was pretty troubled—alcoholic, estranged parents, a mother who was severely depressed and eventually died of alcohol-induced dementia, a sister who to this day does not communicate with me—all of which, my experience told me, was part of the package of the nuclear family. That is, the whole idea of family has always given me trouble, because for me family was the source of my greatest pain. So when I found myself partnered up with a woman who was hell-bent on having a child, and was a midwife besides, I decided, not without real psychic challenges, to let things go in that direction. Actually, I said let's have five years together, and if we make it we'll have a kid. Five years later, we decided to go for it. And now, of course, I fall in love with every kid I see, and I see this as the greatest gift I've ever received.

How do you see parenting as a political act?
I see every act as political, and parenting more than most. If politics is about the use and management of social power, then what could be more political than the decision to take responsibility for another human being? The decision to intentionally help shape another's life and have ones' own life shaped in return; the commitment to engage in community at the level necessary for child-rearing, to engage in education, the commitment to self-consciously help direct another person's experience of the world, and to share the most profound aspects of humanity. And, if radical politics is about challenging concentrations of power, and promoting ethical action—which I believe it is—then parenting is about imparting ethical beliefs, and engaging on a daily basis with the praxis of transforming "power-over"—coercive power—into "power-with"—shared, social power. By the way, my daughter's three, so "praxis" might be a big word here.

I am very interested in hearing about your attempt to integrate your role as a parent and an activist (both successfully and unsuccessfully); or how has parenting informed your activism?
Given that Sacha is barely three, I wouldn't

say there's tremendous integration, except to the extent that I am an activist living and working in a community of activists, so there is a shared commitment among those we parent with, to do things in a way that is consistent with our beliefs. Sacha's mom is a midwife, which is a tremendous form of community service, personal, spiritual service, and activism, so doing my best to support that, is part of it too. And, for better or worse, my work—my activism—involves international travel. I advocate and document struggles for environmental human rights at an international level—so balancing my travel, my partner's midwifery, and raising a child as attentively as possible—it ain't easy, but its all part of the commitment to making the world a better place. And yes, failure to get it right is definitely a part of it—which, honestly, can be refreshing in a world where we're so programmed against failure of any sort. But that's where the growth happens, isn't it?

So, how has parenting informed my activism? It's cliché, but it's true that it gives my work deeper meaning. Soon after Sacha was born I remember thinking—I spent most of my youth and young adulthood feeling angry—politically angry, personally angry. I finally worked past a lot of that anger while still engaging in the work of fighting injustice, and now, I'm going to be angry all over again. Because when you see failing schools, laws targeting youth, toxic chemicals everywhere, in everything, and the tremendous insensitivity of this country and this world to the most basic of human needs, and when you're seeing that in the light of your own child's needs, it is extremely difficult—for me, anyway—to not get mad and then to want to take action. And…especially internationally, I find that people take me and my work more seriously because I'm a parent. As my partner said to me during the difficult transition into parenthood, "Welcome to the human race." I think when people know you are handling something beyond your own more-or-less-selfish interests, something that everyone knows is extremely difficult and yet driven by fierce personal commitment, it automatically generates respect, which builds connection, which is, simply put, good for organizing.

And of course, let's not forget the love. The love you feel for your child is so profound, so transformative, so encompassing, that it touches everything you do. If your work is to influence the workings of the world, then a superabundance of love is bound to have some positive impact on that work, and ideally that love gets spread to some degree through the work.

What is your most humbling moment as a parent?

That is a terrible question. All those moments rush to compete with each other in the front of my brain. There are a lot of proud moments—beginning with having caught my daughter when she was born. But humbling, or worse—humiliating moments—there are many. They almost always have to do with wanting to do something other than attend immediately to the child's needs, and maybe being in a frustrating moment with my partner, and getting angry beyond reason. There were a few times, at least a few, where the baby was screaming and I was screaming too because managing the situation was beyond me. At one of those moments, this was perhaps the very worst, I was alone with my daughter and she was maybe six months old, and she wouldn't stop hollering, and I threw something, a spoon I think, across the kitchen and it hit a drinking glass and the glass shattered, and suddenly I have a screaming baby and broken glass everywhere and I am damn lucky there was no injury. And, you know, after a moment like that everything seems to get real quiet, and you take a deep breath, and you clean up the glass and soothe the baby and by the time you're done you're in a different mood altogether. So, yeah, every truly humbling moment seems to be about my needs being in competition with the child's needs – and when you are suddenly forced to realize that you're competing with a one-year old, that I think is the very definition of humbling.

In what ways do you see fathers as nurturers?
Fatherhood is an opportunity to nurture, and I think men need these opportunities—not to impress, not to give because you're going to get something back, but to simply, deeply, sweetly, care for that child. It is a very healing role to play, and a wonderful way to spend time on this earth. And of course there are many ways to nurture—play can be nurture, teaching, reading aloud, or just holding the child. Sometimes I think one of the most nurturing things is not to do what we think of as nurturing, you know, soothing and saying "It's okay, dada's here," but to say, "What's it like for you? What are you experiencing right now?" Which is, of course, not what men in general are raised to do.

How does the issue of race come up in your parenting?
Both my partner and I are white, and we're both acutely aware of our white privilege, and of the harm of racism, and we share a strong desire, which I think we fulfill pretty well, to raise our daughter in multi-racial, multi-cultural settings. But we're also acutely aware that the choice and ability to do that is founded in our privilege; challenging racism is not just about exposure to other cultures, obviously, but about breaking down stereotypes and arbitrary power dynamics and so on. How do we do that with our daughter? It's still early to talk with her about this sort of thing—potty training is enough of a psychic burden—but we hope that, by being openly surrounded by people with as wide a variety of skin shades and languages and cultures as possible—and the Bay Area is certainly a great place for that—that this will lead to a natural understanding that all people are created equal and are worthy of respect and friendship and love. And we build on it from there to help her understand the damage that racism causes. How do we deal with whiteness itself—the fact that it's an arbitrary category of power in which she, by virtue of being born into it, is a de facto participant? It'll be a lifelong process, as it is with us, no?

How is your parenting different from the way you've been parented? And what can explain the change?
When I was born my father was 45 years old and had three kids from another marriage. He was an ex-Marine who'd fought in World War II, and was a recovered alcoholic. My mother was an un-recovered alcoholic who smoked while I was in the womb and found the idea of breastfeeding—I learned later—"disgusting." From very young until high school I watched 6 hours of TV each day, ate junk food, and played video games. In short, "conscious parenting" was not on the agenda. That said, mom was an editor and dad was a good-guy lawyer, both democrats with liberal politics around race and other issues. My mother integrated my Little League—this is the mid-seventies—by demanding that the town provide buses to bring black kids from across town.

My partner and I make great effort to gauge the kind of input our daughter is getting, engage her in creative play, teach her the value of healthy food, be open, honest, loving, and attentive. I think the difference has a generational aspect—we are informed by feminism, by the men's movement, by things like therapy and alternative health and organics that barely existed in the seventies, for older parents especially. There's also an aspect that my partner and I make great effort not to repeat what we see as our parents' mistakes—for my part that includes extraordinary effort to not be like them, because they served as such negative role models. I think my parents were still of a generation where having kids and a family was just what you did—it wasn't a question of choice. Since we have chosen to become parents, that brings with it an ideal of choosing what kind of parents to be.

What's your favorite book to read or story to tell with your child right now? Other recommendations?

When I read her The Lorax—which I do often—I think, "what more is there to say on this subject? Doesn't that cover it?" A book I love is called The Bear That Wasn't, about a bear who hibernates only to wake up in the spring and find that a factory was built over his cave. When he leaves the cave, he's told to get to work, and he can't seem to convince the managers that he's a bear—"You're just a silly man who needs a shave and wears a fur coat, now get to work!" they tell him. He ends up believing them and when the factory shuts down and winter comes again, he sits there and nearly freezes to death until he remembers that he's a bear, and goes back into his cave. What a great story! And then there are all the books she loves that you've gotta go along with. Dora the Explorer and all that. Dora's kind of a technogeek, but I guess that's cool for a girl, and at least she speaks Spanish. I really enjoyed your book about how the Zapatistas use storytelling and mythology to create their identity, to in fact make their dreams a reality; in what ways has studying the Zapatistas and working with them taught you about family or about parenting or raising children.

One of the most essential things I learned in the few years I worked in Zapatista communities is summed up in something a Zapatista friend said to me once: "Our struggle is not for us, but for our grandchildren." Despite the urgency to address injustice and oppression right now, being indigenous, the Zapatistas take the long view, and they taught me that, not only do things rarely change overnight, the greatest results of our work are not necessarily even seen in our lifetimes. Could anything be more true of parenthood than that?

Secondly—the mythology—all the language the Zapatistas use to bring their ideologies to life can, in some ways, be invoked by one word that they use a lot—dignity. Dignity, for the Zapatistas, means the right and the ability to live to one's full potential. If anything radical is at the heart of my own parenting, it is a desire to raise my daughter with that sense of revolutionary dignity—that she should have that, and the she should impart it to others.

Interview with JonJon Cassagnol

by Art Noose, Pittsburgh PA

JonJon Cassagnol is a musician and father living in Pittsburgh, PA. You will soon be able to hear his music on his website jonjoncassagnol.com. Interview conducted by Artnoose, who also lives in Pittsburgh.

What was your own growing up like, in a multicultural city?
My young adolescence was in New York and then I moved to Miami. It was nice to be in a melting pot of many cultures there. The area I grew up in was predominantly black, and it was a relatively rough neighborhood called Richmond Heights. And it has "Heights" in the name so you know how it is. And although it was a bad neighborhood, there was a sense of community there. I felt like it was a good place for me to grow up, because I had that urban environment and I also had the Latino influence that Miami has to offer.

What languages did you hear growing up?
We spoke Haitian at home, but mostly everyone spoke Spanish in Miami. Maybe in one city you might have one Spanish radio station but there you had a handful. There were three or four radio stations. And you had Haitian radio stations as well—non-existent in most places. And Haitian restaurants, so I was also able to enjoy food from Haiti as well in Miami.

And you grew up with just your mom?
Just my mother, yes.

Any other relatives?
My family in the Haitian culture is like any other Caribbean culture—my family was always on tour. My mother, when she would go to Haiti, would stay with her sisters, and they have the house that they all stayed in. Growing up at home I always had aunts and uncles and family that would be coming through and staying at the house. So in a sense I had many influences as far as parenting is concerned. And my mom worked a lot.

Eventually you became a punk on the West Coast, and I feel like that's an unusual trajectory—you know—a son of immigrant Haitians in Miami is suddenly a punk in San Francisco. How did that happen?

I learned that you didn't need to be financially stable to travel and check out the world. I ended up on the west coast pursuing music, and it just happened by coincidence that I was on the west coast. In New Orleans I'd met a lot of people from the west coast and I wound up traveling out there and living a little adventure.

How old were you?
I was seventeen. I left high school to do this. I wanted to eventually move to New York and go to school, but first I felt an urgency to see the world. In my community in Miami I felt extremely supported—like it was overly supportive. It gave me this huge confidence that maybe I was more than I was. Once I checked out New Orleans and saw the world a little I realized I'm not a perfect person. I thought I was great and all that stuff, but my little bubble was burst at that time. I left to the west coast to soul search. I ended up in San Francisco. I lived in Golden Gate Park for about six months, did some traveling in the northwest and moved back to New Orleans.

At some point you met Wendy. What was your life like when you both decided to have a kid, and what was that discussion like?
I got back to Florida and then we met. She had a whole bunch of friends that traveled. I came back from four years of traveling straight. We were friends for many months before a spark happened and then we just continued traveling. We traveled for about two years straight, and then we decided to settle down and have a child. So we moved back and tried to have a child for a year and finally it happened. We were living in Ohio.

When you were having that conversation, did you ever talk about what would happen if you separated?

We were so young. I was twenty two. It was one of those dreams that you have that you'll never separate from this person. Especially when you spend every day together for two years straight—planning this life with someone. I've realized that you can grow apart—especially when you're building the core person of who you are.

Did you have any ideas about what parenting would be like that didn't end up being like how you thought they would?

I didn't think there would be a television in the house, although there isn't one here so when she comes over here it's nice, but I never thought that the internet would, you know—I didn't grow up with internet. I wasn't nine years old with internet. Gizzy is online. She has a FaceBook. These things I didn't take into account in regards to being a certain way. I thought the influence of American culture would be easier to block. That's the hardest part—there's so much outside influence.

Is there anything that was how you thought it would be?
I knew I would be supportive of what she wants to do and to be able to communicate with her as an adult but also as a friend. I knew I would be more of a parent than either of my parents were—just the social dynamic that I grew up in. I grew up first generation American.

After you and Wendy separated, how did you make the decision to come to Pittsburgh to be closer to your daughter?
We were both living in Florida, and when we separated—thank god for the very supportive family that she has. They gave me the support to be close to them and continue parenting. I had an amazing career in Miami that was very hard to build. It was kind of heartbreaking to leave that, but I knew it was for the best. I stayed in Florida for about six or seven months to save some money and I looked at a map, which seems to be the main thing I do when I have a major life change. I looked at a map and saw Cleveland and Columbus. Then I

saw Pennsylvania and I had never thought I would live in Pittsburgh—or even visit. I had never been here before. I thought it would be a great adventure, and it was fueled by being closer to Gizzy. My decision to move to Pittsburgh, a city I had never been to, would probably be the best decision I've ever made. And that's what my gut told me. And it was. This is my new home, and it's about forty-five minutes away from where she lives. Pittsburgh happened to be closer than any other city was.

What are some of the challenges to parenting a child who lives in different city?
It's not as hard as I thought it would be, because we are very close. It gets a little hectic if I have to go to a school function, and scheduling for work. You know, going to her gymnastics performances. For me, the difficulty is not being able to see her—I wouldn't even say on a daily basis—but on a weekly basis. I feel like I'm able to see her on a bi-weekly basis, which is not the greatest but it's a lot better than bimonthly, like when I was living in Florida. It's nice to live closer. I'd love to move to Ohio but that's never going to happen. I don't think I would be able to afford it. The best alternative I have is to live in Pittsburgh.

Do your ever talk to your daughter about your politics?
Yeah, especially now that we have a black president. I tell her that it's important to have her own opinion and not to be influenced by her friends, what's cool, or what's not cool.

You have a number of queer friends—do you ever talk to your daughter about homophobia?
She asked me once what I thought about two

guys holding hands. I explained to her that when you're an adult you can make these decisions, and it's natural as long as you're happy with it, and that there's absolutely nothing wrong with it. I don't bring religion in it. She's a Baptist and homosexuality is frowned upon there.

Does your daughter have much exposure to Haitian culture/people in her daily life? How do you and your family introduce that kind of culture—music, food, language, stories, travel, history, etc? I'm assuming there isn't a Haitian population in the town where she lives.

No, there isn't a Haitian population there. There is one in Pittsburgh, though. Since the earthquake in Haiti, she's been seeing a lot of pictures, and hearing a lot in regards to that. Her Haitian culture happens about twice a year, when we take our summer and winter vacations. The other side of her family is full Hungarian, so she's getting a lot of influence on that side. Although she doesn't speak Creole—which would be nice—I'm making that her own decision. When I grew up in a Haitian family, I was more concerned about being American, and I knew that there was a cultural gap and a language barrier. I guess the Haitian earthquake has brought a lot of Haitian influence into her life because she knows that she has family there that she's concerned about. It's that and Haitian cooking. She thinks the language is pretty cool and might want to learn French in school.

Are there ways you have felt supported by your friends/comrades here in Pittsburgh specifically with regards to being a parent? Are there ways in which you would have liked more or different support?

There aren't a lot of parents around, although more in Pittsburgh than any city I've seen there are a lot of kid-friendly events. You can go to a punk rock show in Pittsburgh and see kids with big ear protection. On flyers I'm seeing more and more notes saying it's kid-friendly. There should be more of that in other cities. I think that Pittsburgh is very supportive in that way. If more people had kids, then maybe everything will be more kid-friendly!

Do you have any advice for new fathers?

My advice to new fathers is to re-evaluate the people you associate with. When you are a father, the people you know will tie into that, and it will be knit into the fabric of your future. Think about the person you want to be and associate yourself with people who are loving and have a healthy lifestyle. That has to begin as soon as you find out that you're having a child, because those things will eventually catch up with you.

Heroes for my Daughter: The Jane Collective

by Jake Jones-Martinez

From 1969 until the 1973 Supreme Court decision Roe v. Wade legalized abortion, Jane counseled women about abortion and helped gain access to underground abortion providers. Jane initially sought to screen abortionists and find competent providers but felt that as long as women are dependent on providers they remain powerless.

Officially known as The Abortion Counseling Service of Women's Liberation and operating in Chicago, the collective counseled women of every class, race, and ethnicity and offered services at little to no cost and no one was turned away for lack of payment. The members of Jane believed reproductive control was essential for their liberation, therefore it was critical that every woman who came to Jane must understand the active role she was taking in her life. To do that, she must be in control of the procedure. The members of Jane realized the only way this could successfully be accomplished was for Jane to control every step of the procedure. Every woman who came to Jane for an abortion was included and in control. She was not a passive recipient of a procedure. In a situation where many women feel powerless, Jane sought to give each woman a sense of her own power, in hopes that she could take back her body, and by extension—her life.

Following in the footsteps of the Underground Railroad and sit-ins at lunch counters throughout the south, the group members deliberately and actively broke the law to set others free. Because simply providing information about abortion was illegal, Jane was the code name for the group and its members. Few, if any, records were kept, and the collective chose not to record the minutes of meetings.

At a time when 5,000 women died each year from complications relating to illegal abortions, not a single woman served by Jane died. More than 12,000 abortions were performed for roughly $25 each, and no one who couldn't pay was turned away.

In her memoir, The Story of Jane, Laura Kaplan, a member of Jane wrote, "Those of us who were members of Jane were remarkable only because we chose to act with women's needs as our guide. In doing so we transformed illegal abortion from a dangerous sordid experience into one that was life affirming and powerful."

In May of 1972, Jane was raided and 7 of its members were arrested. In 1973, after Roe became effective in Illinois the charges were dropped and their records expunged. The collective disbanded shortly thereafter. It is this sort of history that we must keep talking about, keep sharing with each other and our children, lest each new generation comes to believe our freedoms have been given to us by 9 men in black robes. Emma Goldman said, "Liberty will not descend to a people, a people must raise themselves to liberty."

Prayer for Oscar Grant*

by Cyrus Armajani

There is no God but God
no Salt but Salt.
There is no Gun but Warm
no Bullet but Bone.
There is no Glass but Crack
No Crack but Crack.
No Butcher no father.

There is no Water but War
no War but Loss.
There is no Door but Wall
where Wall is Sky
Sky is Car
Car is Fire
There is no Fire but Mountain
Mountain without Streams.

*Twenty-two years old, unarmed, black, a father and a butcher's apprentice, Oscar Grant was murdered in Oakland by Bay Area transit police in the early morning of January 1, 2009.

We Remember Oscar Grant

by Tomas Moniz

It was an accident that I hopped on the wrong train heading back to the East Bay lost as I was in the gallery of Sunday characters riding BART: tourists, hipsters, workers, and young teens. I smiled at them, especially the teenagers, excused their loudness—their energy. I imagined my teenaged daughters and son acting a little crazy just like them on the BART.

As we slipped past West Oakland station, I began to close my book, gather my belongings, but when we pulled into the Lake Merritt station and not 12th street I was confused. I realized I had boarded the wrong train. On or off? I couldn't decide in time, and the doors closed.

No biggie; I'd just get off at the next stop. Which was Fruitvale.

I froze right there.

The skyline swept into view as we emerged from the tunnel, late afternoon sun spilling over the port of Oakland—serene and blinding.
It hit me then: Fruitvale BART station—the place where Oscar Grant was murdered. His murder has stuck with me since it happened on New Year's Eve 2009. I have been to vigils. I have facilitated discussions in classrooms and at Rad Dad readings. I have refused to forget for the last year and a half the violence that is consistently perpetrated on the youth in our society—especially youth of color; especially young men.

But I have not come to where it happened.

The train hummed to a stop and I stepped off. The platform was empty, barren—almost peaceful. The geography was familiar—the cement walls, the red tile flooring.
Immediately, those bumpy, pixilated cell

phone images come to mind, and then the noise, the chaos.

It was nighttime.

There were kids along those walls.

There were cops strong-arming and stomping back and forth.

There was Oscar Grant pushed face down on to the ground.

Then there was the shot.

Standing in the Fruitvale BART station, I couldn't help but feel my chest well up with such emotions—such sadness, such anger. I searched for the spot thinking there must be a memorial: candles, pictures, flowers, something.

But there was nothing.

No sign to mark the spot, no image to bear witness—everything wiped clean. I wonder what is left behind?

I walked the platform.

Soon, the first train heading my direction arrived. Two young men stepped off, laughing, holding cell phones to their ears. They nodded at me and walked to the stairs.

I was alone again and felt that I should do something.

But then I saw it; someone had written something in black sharpie, on the railing.

"We remember."

I remember this as I, like so many in the Bay Area, await the verdict that will most-likely come out in the next few days. Initially, I was nervous, but sure that justice would be served. Nothing could bring back Oscar Grant, nothing could give his daughter her father back, but at least a message would be sent to other officers of the law.

Now, I am not so sure this will happen.

I don't know how I will respond to the verdicts.

I fear the police are all too ready to subdue, to quell, to brutalize.

But they will not scare me away.

One thing I do know is that my daughters and I will be there with other people in downtown Oakland the evening the verdict is released.

I know we will not forget.

What the Nightly News Didn't Show You About Mehserle Verdict Protest

by Tehea Robie

One mother's response to the Verdict interspersed with voices of those speaking on the corner of 14th and Broadway. Many of the first speakers were sobbing through their words.

Rage is the type of thing you can't really plan for.

You can board up windows, fill the sky with helicopters, televise warnings of terrifying riot-Armageddon—but you can't actually anticipate that emotion. Most of us don't feel it until the acid curdle of our own blood boils, till we feel like ripping off clothes and letting gargantuan green selves emerge, Incredible Hulk style. I am the white mother of two black sons, and I'm angry. My kids have two or three more years before they stop looking like little kids, and start looking like targets, like "criminals" to the media and the white infrastructure that surrounds them. I'm running a race to change the world before that happens. Before the stopwatch stops...before my babies become involuntary suspects for crooked cops.

Tyisha: "My heart is hurting so bad right now, I can't even focus. These people think that they can instantly come and get the youth to follow them, like it's a band, like it's hella cute to be out here, like we just out here playing at this. I'm so tired of going to funerals, I swear. Makes no sense that the police can continue to kill people, day after day.

"Involuntary manslaughter, are you serious? Are you serious? I just lost three partners in three months. All senior graduates. Nobody's been arrested for their murders. Police out here like they're actually doing something. Oh, police are going to get laid off, oh, let's go help them. Are you fucking serious? I'm sorry children, for cussing, but this is how I feel. Saving them for what? They're not saving us! "My 'lil partner got killed near Eastmont Mall, right across the street from the police station! Right across the street. {stops and sobs} It don't make no sense! I haven't seen a helicopter in Oakland in five years. In five years! Who is saving the youth? Who is saving the youth? Nobody! We don't have programs for these kids, they got nothing to do! They tear up downtown, don't even know what's going on. They don't even know the truth. They don't even know their history. They don't know who Emmett Till was, 14 years old. And he got murdered. And those people got to walk free. "{Mehserle trial} They got a new juror in what, a weekend? Oh, I'm sick. Oh, I'm going on vacation. Involuntary manslaughter. "I'm so tired. I swear. I'm only 20 years old, and I'm so tired."

I didn't know the extent of my anger about the Johannes Mehserle verdict. I didn't know until I got downtown, to the site of the community gathering organized by Oakland General Assembly for Justice for Oscar Grant. The sound system wasn't set up yet; the disorganized scene resulted in an impromptu call to march. It was 5:40 p.m. Most of the people there took to the street.

Sherri: "I'm a little bit nervous, because it's just
a lot of stuff. I've been having dreams. I think God is telling me to say something or do something. I have a son to worry about. I'm really hurt to my heart that we don't have unity amongst ourselves. I keep feeling like we're gonna die out, like the natives, like the Indians of America. I keep having that fear. I wish we had more self pride. Oh my god. {crying, stops} We seem like lost causes already. Let that baby die in the hospital. Let the school close down. We don't have enough unity so of course we're gonna seem like lost causes for somebody else to kill. "Stop being quick to kill your own brother! You might be from the same tribe or something! Stop being quick to look at your own sister crazy! Stop dividing

your own family! We are not each other's enemy. God says fear no man. The policeman is a human being. Why are we fearing them? I'm not about to look up my poem right now, but the poem is called 'Red Carpet' because we keep sweeping this shit under the rug. Racism is real, it's not going nowhere. Stop sweeping it under the rug."

I was livid. I was thinking about the fact that nearly hundreds of police and National Guard were about to meet up with a crowd that had no previous civil disobedience plan. I cussed out innocent bystanders and orange-vested "peace-makers" from the mayor's office, demanding to know where the rally's organizers were.   That's when the amps went live and the crowd swelled. I heard a young woman crying on the mic. She called me back to my senses. We can't plan for the feeling of rage, but we can train ourselves to act right. Rage is unprocessed grief. When it's let out the right way, it's more powerful than tear gas, or rubber bullets.
For me, this is the real news about the protest on the eve of the Grant verdict, no matter what you heard. I witnessed a peaceful protest begin and end in peace. I walked home in peace. When I got home, I heard about all the rest. I couldn't sleep until I saw that the Rachel Maddow Show had covered the verdict.

Hannibal: "So I know everyone is upset about how the United Snakes of America chose to deal with this particular murder ... but you should not expect justice to come from an unjust system. You cannot expect the police to charge themselves with murder, when they do that as a business. They are diametrically opposed to us being treated as equals. The only thing that we can gain as a community, out of this particular case, is to look around at each other, to see who really has your back. To see who's really down for you, when it comes down to the fight, right? The only justice that we're gonna see in this case, is gonna come from the people that I'm looking at right here in front

me: "You should know about Gary King Jr. You should know about Anita Gay. You should know about Andrew Moppin. And know that this thing has been going on as long as there has been such thing as America. And know that the only way we're gonna get out of it, is when we look at each other and realize that we're going to have come up with our own solutions. We need to develop our own community system, based on the well being of each and every member of our community. So when you put pressure on these courts, just keep in mind, it's only to wake your brother and your sister up."

Picking Our Battles

by Renee Cashmere

Many of the truths I try to teach my girls are obvious. The ones that aren't as obvious seem to be the biggest influence on our lives right now. They repeatedly crisscross and parallel all over our paths no matter how much we try to ignore them. A constant struggle for me has been compromise and boundaries and living with myself after reacting to perceived offense. My initial reaction to challenging situations is rage. I rarely cry and my daughters rarely see it happen, but I often slip into very quiet, articulate anger. After waging battle I often feel guilty about the sharpness of my anger and am physically exhausted. Lately it's occurred to me my daughters see me fighting all the time and I wonder if I'm doing them any favors with this example.

I'm trying to refine what I'm going to teach them about compromise because I still don't know how to do it myself: when to stick to my guns and when to let things go, how anger can fuel but it can also corrode. There's a time for activism and a time to walk away. The past few years for us have been about survival. I was raised by activist parents and pride myself on these values, but I do not have enough in me to fight these days. Sometimes my guilt about this is minor, like when I use paper plates because I'm too dead tired to do another load of dishes. Sometimes it's all consuming because it feels so hugely wrong but seems too big to change.

When the school year began I disliked my daughters' 3rd grade teacher almost immediately. I'm very protective over my girls—that's my job. This lady makes me instantly go to my bad place, temper-wise. I think she sees discipline as the number one way to teach. She gives an hour to an hour and a half of homework a day. These kids are 8. I'm a single mom and work full time, and this much homework is not going to happen. The teacher began keeping my daughter in at recess to make her finish the homework. I had a mommy rage moment. I told her we'd do up to 45 minutes a night—no more—and there would be no retribution. Period. Many parents have complained about this teacher. I'm pro-union but I know the teachers' union is mightier than any group of complaints and a teacher less than a decade from retirement would never be fired based on performance. I was told by another mom that news of putting my foot down on the homework issue travelled throughout the land and playground amongst the other moms and it was a bit of juicy gossip in my predominantly stay-at-home neighborhood.

While my daughter is at school I'm at work for a public official elected by the voters of the state of California. I hate my job. Let's establish that I am thankful to have a job. What enrages me on a daily basis is how this economy has not only affected those who don't have jobs, but how those who do have jobs are treated. On a large scale level, this bureaucracy I work in is broken. It's broken to the point that I believe it's not possible to fix it—it has to be razed and recreated from scratch. On a smaller scale the wonderful people I work with on a daily basis are wasted resources. Their intelligence, skills and personalities are eventually punished and squandered on every level. Last month I went to a conference where the public official I work for was the keynote speaker. Part of his speech was about his belief that all politicians should do as he does, and get to know all the departments and employees under him on a personal level. I sat in my work clothes and lipstick and burned with anger at the irony.

So the truth I've been trying to put into words for my girls lately is to stand your ground, but know when to walk away. The politicians I work for puts food on our table and a roof over our heads. When my daughter tells me she doesn't like her teacher, I tell her she needs to make it work. I tell her these lessons are good opportunities to learn how to find a comfortable place between standing up for ourselves and letting it go peacefully as possible. It's about asking for compassion from others but not basing everything we are upon getting it. We have to fight, but first we have to preserve ourselves and the people we love and are responsible for.

I want my daughters to be activists, but I know how important it is to conserve energy and pick your battles, especially when emotion is involved. I don't want them to be fighting and angry all the time. I've taught them so much about standing up for themselves and what they believe in, but ultimately I just want them to have peace. If they can't have peace in their everyday world I want them to at least have peace in their minds and home.

Fierce Love

by Loi Medvin

I love my daughter with a fierceness that has no equal. Ever since she was born, my heart has grown larger. Sometimes it aches with that growth and contracts in pain, sometimes it expands in joy. But always, even in our darkest, most hateful moments, there is still that connection. It is a cord that connects us, and it always will bind us together, no matter how far she will go away from me.

These adolescent years seem the hardest. In the past, when things were difficult, she would still cuddle up to me at night, turn to me when she was hurting, trusting me to make it all better. But now, she turns away and even hurts herself. How can I—who vowed to protect her with all my life—protect her from the crushing world? How can I protect her from her adolescent, hormonal reactions to a misogynistic and confusing society? How can I encourage that strong and brilliant little girl to continue growing, to continue knowing that she is wonderful? How can I remind her that girls—that women are potent as they are, inherently beautiful and powerful without using their bodies as weapons, as tools to get what they need? How can I help her understand how amazing she is inside and what a gift to us all she is, when she is pushing away from me?

It is the separation of adolescence, the individuation time and so mostly when I speak, she discounts my voice. I know she must find her own way, but it's so difficult when she maybe doesn't even recognize her own voice, and so denies it. With that denial, comes a denial of her own unique worth, and our culture not only agrees, but fosters this betrayal of purity and trust, of integrity and soul so that she will become a good little consumer, a follower of the flock, one of the sheep.

I pray she wakes up soon to the beauty of her inner self and remembers the joy that this world also has to offer. But until this time, I hold this vision for my daughter and will remind her in both subtle and forward ways, of the true power of who she is. I hold this until she will reclaim it because I must—I protect her as I can, I love her without limits, because I am her mother.

Artist Mama

by Tyler Cohen

My daughter just turned 5 and I have to admit, in these early years, I've had a lot less time for my work—I'm a lot less productive. I bemoaned this for quite some time, looking at the lives of free-floating others with envy and a sense of loss. I look back to other artists and found the ones able to devote their full lives to their work were usually childless, had a wife or a nanny—if rich—to raise their young, or were absent and/or crazy. Where are the artists who are adoringly raising their offspring while pursuing their inner drives and visions? Is it possible? A while back I read somewhere that collectors don't like to collect/invest in artists who are mothers. That pissed me off—why should an artist's work be less valued because she is a mother? It screams of sexism.

Flash to the morning of the first day of Zine Fest this past year. Zine Fest is the primary way I've been getting my work out these last few years. This year I was coming with new and different work and I was anxious to reveal it to others and receive feedback. I was rushing to get myself and my stuff out the door and to the Fest on time. I came out of the bathroom to find my daughter with cream cheese smeared all over her hands and a good part of her face—she had obviously been busy while I showered and my partner slept. My partner, too, is spread thin: he's a student, frequently up until all-hours in order to make progress on his projects. I had to help her get cleaned up before I left. I am sorry but I admit—there was yelling involved. She was playing; that's what kids do, but I was trying to get my work out the door—our needs were, at that moment, in conflict. How to be an artist mama and not a struggling mama-struggling artist?

The need to take advantage of narrower windows of time has lead me to adjust my media use. I'm currently working more with colored pencils more than with the brush and inks I'd been using previously because there is no setup or clean up time involved. I miss the feel of brush and ink on paper, however, and pull them out once in a while—only to later chisel the hardened abandoned ink out of the pallet. Like the combinations of pencil and ink I've produced and assume that this means my work is growing, or at least changing—I can only hope in a way that is engaging to viewer/readers. I often wish I were one of those people who can regularly get by with little sleep.

And then, there's the need for money. Art and commerce have a confused and confusing relationship for me. I believe I have a purpose in what I do, that it is something that I must do. That art is a gift and responsibility. But I also need a roof—I need to eat and care for my family. My work has never sold well—much better as books than as drawings. I have been told by many that it is beautiful, interesting, scary, but it will never be the kind of work that will decorate. Nonetheless, I found my voice in the world of the Primazons—the worlds I create—and pleasure in the craft. Primazons and Primazonia are a people and world through which I explore, express, and find my query into the complicated and even contradictory qualities that I perceive as making up female animal relationships, the spasmodic expressions of nature and nurture, dominance, play, destruction and connectivity. I am driven, too, by the feeling that if we do not address the ape-animal that is a part of who we are, we will not be able to heal many of the destructive and unhealthful forms of human relationships and cultural relationships. I strive to make drawn narratives that are not yet determined moments, accessed through tension and beauty to draw the viewer/reader into complicity with Primazonia. I love to draw and can be good at it. In it I find pleasure and challenge, a place for examination, observation, meditation, and a place for query. Time that should go to this work gets diverted to paying gigs.

It's a struggle. For time, for focus, and for energy—the relentlessness of even the most basic of home maintenance, healthy food, and child care on top of paid work. But retaining a hold on the value of my art, or my art practice and play is worth it. I think of my grandmothers' generation of bright, intelligent women, dampened, bound, unhappy—and how they passed their unhappiness on. I can forget to find space for myself—and this is when I lose my balance. But when I do find that space, there is more of me to bring back to my family. After spending time on my work, I am more grounded and able to be present with my child and my partner. My mood is better—I feel whole, accomplished, and not torn and distracted by conflicting needs and desires, freeing my spirit to feel playful. Because that is also what art is: play—and we all need proper playtime to free our minds, bodies and spirits, to keep our minds elastic, creative, crafty, and, ultimately, joyful.

I have received benefits, too, in the union of artist and mama. I've gotten to directly observe my own little Primazon daughter and her cohort, adding to the Primazonia narrative(s), expanding the universe, yet remaining true to my query. I get to share the joys of making things, of color and line, pattern, book-making and character-making with my daughter; and I have even been inspired by things she's doing in her own amazing work—she is astoundingly prolific. So, my work has grown; it's just a matter of the amount of time I actually have to produce anything. My daughter has grown too. Last night, she had her first sleepover at a friends. Not only did I get to sleep in until 10 a.m., I got to have a morning cuddle and muss the sheets with my partner, and here I am with a moment to write this. She's busier with school; in the last six months I've been able to produce nearly 50 pages of storyboards and three larger three-color drawings—a big change over previous years.

I am trying to have a different attitude these days, trying to integrate these selves: artist, mother, worker. To be an artist mama, who is good at designing books and visual communication—and tries to find people who will pay her to do it. And let's not forget being a partner and lover, friend, and dreamer. To be whole. I believe that my work has value and I keep making it, even at my slowed pace, with the determination of blind faith. I know that for those who connect with what I create, the work/the product has value, too.

The Handsome Daughter

by Lauren Pretnar

One of the first issues that arose during my pregnancy was whether or not we were going to find out the baby's sex before birth. I didn't especially want to but my partner did, and when he suggested half-jokingly that he could find out and keep it to himself I decided to go ahead and ruin the surprise with him. We'd find out eventually anyway, he rationalized; what would a few months earlier or later change? I'm pretty sure it's about the method of discovery and not the timing, but anyway...

Once I'd signed on, I looked forward to the possibility of the baby not crossing its legs during our one ultrasound. I had wanted to wait partly because I love surprises and partly because I didn't want to give false weight to our child's male or female-ness. In the end, I realized that our excitement didn't stem from a specific desire to know the sex of our child but a general desire to know something. We had no interest in stocking up on gender-specific clothes and toys and decorations for a nursery ahead of time, no need to narrow down baby names as soon as possible; we just wanted a piece of concrete information around which we could daydream for the second half of my pregnancy.

Still, there's no escaping it. Gender and all its weird trappings rear their heads even before birth and keep on rearing once the baby arrives, whether or not the mama consents.

Gender is a hugely challenging and endlessly intriguing topic, and more often than not I am infuriated by the way gender expectations play out in my life, the lives of my loved ones, and society as a whole.

Having a little girl has taught me that boy = infant neutral. Babies, with their no hair or short hair, are assumed to be male barring the conspicuous addition of some explicitly feminine indicator/signal. My daughter is mistaken over and over again for a boy even when wearing mildly feminine garb. At ten months, she is now beginning to cultivate enough hair to be automatically perceived by some as female. I'm sure there are female babies that somehow look particularly like little girls without any extra adornment, but I'm also sure that they are in the vast minority.

Given this early androgyny amongst the baby set, it's surprisingly rare for strangers to come right out and ask, "Boy or girl?" I had always assumed that the only reason parents would dress their babies in nothing but boringly explicit "gender-appropriate" clothing is because they themselves are utterly unimaginative. While this might be true in many cases, after the first dozen consecutive times that my neutrally-dressed daughter was taken for a boy, I amended my judgment to include parents who find it disturbing to have their child mistaken for the opposite sex. Then, one particularly exhausted morning, I caught myself sorting through my daughter's baby clothes in search of something identifiably girly. Upon self-cross-examination, I realized that we had to go out and run errands and I didn't feel like dealing with the irritation of strangers.

Which leads me to lesson number two. I enjoy dressing my child in all sorts of clothes and I don't have any problem with her being mistaken for a boy, but strangers often grow offended and irritated if they can't guess the sex of my child. Gender-specific clothing is a social shortcut that allows strangers to gracefully apply pronouns and adjectives to an infant they don't know. It's not just parents who find such such social cues important; lots of people expect parents to offer enough hints for them to make accurate gender assumptions without too much effort. Furthermore, if parents don't do this—especially mothers—since fathers can be forgiven for not knowing how to "properly" dress their children—there will be embarrassment, dirty looks, and even scolding.

I don't know why this surprised me, given

that androgyny and other challenges to gender norms are most often met with extreme discomfort and sometimes even violence. Perhaps I naively assumed that infants would get a pass from society's bizarre intensity around this stuff for at least the first year of their lives. In a way they do, since it's adults who dress them and are either rewarded or punished for their choices. That the weight of such judgments will eventually shift to my daughter—and probably sooner than I imagine—is a reality amongst so many that it gives me the chills.

But for now I can be a buffer. My kid is gorgeous; handsome—the best-looking baby around. Her favorite book this week is "My Little Toolbox" and her favorite toys are a squeaky dog ball, a mirror, and plum-colored sequined tank top that her mother bought a decade ago but never had the guts to wear and so lets her drag around the house. She is lanky and strong, stubborn and charming, and completely unconcerned about making other people comfortable. All she cares about is learning to walk. And soon she'll start picking out her own clothes.

Kids' Noise

by China Martins

In 2005 I toured with Ariel Gore, the founder of HipMama magazine and author of six books. I had never toured before. At each event, Ariel announced that we were OK with kids' noise; our words had, after all, been written in the real life chaos of our lives and so how appropriate that they be read that way as well. Parents should not worry because we could speak over any child. The way she put it always got a laugh and a lot of appreciation.

Later Vikki Law and I used this approach in our "Don't Leave Your Friends Behind" (DLYFB) workshops. We have also made these announcements when we have been speakers and suggested this to others as a way to make a space more child-friendly.

What I personally like to say is that we are glad to see parents and children in the audience, that many times parents are given the "hairy eyeball" if their children make any little sound, and then feel that they must leave and not hear the information. We don't want to do that so we let the audience know that sounds are fine with us, and that we can speak louder to be heard.
We the speakers can deal with it and ask the audience to also. If someone has a problem with some sounds, maybe they should pick up their chair and move to another part of the room rather then thinking the parent and child should. Or perhaps they should offer to take a restless child out of the room so the parent can continue to listen and give input instead of thinking the parent should leave. Giving children attention by including them in the discussion or sharing with them a task they can do—instead of only telling them what they shouldn't do or ignoring them—can help the situation flow smoother as well.

Children's sounds aren't the end of the world. But somehow we have the notion that complete silence is necessary when "important people" speak. However, having more space to yourself can be seen as a huge factor within who is more privileged than another. Many parents cannot afford the complete silence of uninterrupted time and space. Our conversations and planning may go on while juggling other activities, within our discontent on the job, in the corners of the dawn or at the edge of kitchen tables.

Many public activist conversations also have problems with adults—some groups of adults more then others—taking up too much space, talking over each other, and other improper behaviors, but a child just being a child is greeted with a greater amount of anger. What are they doing here? seems to be the reaction. If you don't have a partner, can't afford a babysitter, or don't feel ready/want to be separated from your child—you should stay secluded with them in the children's spaces or at home, and not join us at these talks.
The noise of children is seen as something that is an intrusion on adults. Perhaps is it still the old "seen and not heard" rule.

But it doesn't have to be like this. In different settings, as well as in other cultures and countries, the attitude can be vastly different. Activists who have traveled to Chiapas and spent time with Zapatistas commonly report that children run in and out of the room and are present at every gathering. One person told Vikki that, in addition to children's sounds, sometimes a meeting was interrupted by the sounds of a military helicopter flying overhead: everyone would run out to look; then return to continue the meeting. To this person, although they recognized their own limits and did not want to do childcare personally, the idea of anyone being upset with the sounds of children was absurd!

But often in North America and—it seems to me—most prominently in predominately white middle class spaces, a noise from a child will cause the whole room to turn and give a disapproving look. What usually happens is that the parent's tension rises, they become more militant to suppress or prevent any sound, and when it happens again, they get up, flustered, and leave. Sometimes even in vocally child-friendly spaces a parent will leave something that they have looked forward to and worked hard to get there, feeling like a bad parent, upset and alone, to soothe a fussy child who will not be easily soothed. Parenting is hard work, especially new parenting where one's life is majorly changed and one often does not even get enough uninterrupted sleep. Parents may have to leave a room more frequently than others, but they shouldn't be pushed out before they feel ready to leave.

Recently, Amy told me about trying to make a more child-friendly space at a bookstore reading by bringing blocks to occupy children in the audience. The blocks made sounds and the feeling in the room was like electrified tension. The parent and child left to get away from that.
I remember in our original DLYFB talk—which is geared towards those without children of their own: only a few parents were in the audience. They were struggling with a child playing with fold up chairs. Within our discussion they felt brave enough to bring up their feelings: A parent raised her hand and shared that this was the kind of thing that would cause them to usually leave. We stopped our conversation on hypothetical supporting parents and children situations and started a new group discussion based on what was happening right then: What would be the best way to handle this? What would make this room more friendly and relaxed? The parent said it would be nice for others to make eye contact with them or their children or smile. They are afraid of being an inconvenience to others. From this first discussion came our list of concrete ways to support parents. It seemed a very constructive use of a workshop, to gather and to interact with each other, all different members and needs, not make it some place where only some feel free to speak, though it's important to acknowledge all those who couldn't make it there that day and why.

I remember when I first met a new mom

zine-friend, Connie, who had traveled all the way from Colorado to California on her own with a new baby to meet Jessica Mills, Tomas Moniz, Rahula Jankowski, and I for our book reading in Modern Times Books. I had told her she would have support when she arrived and wanted to make sure that happened. I ran out, maybe a little too enthusiastic, and offered to hold her infant, to give her arms a break, so she could tend to what ever she needed to and listen to our reading. I made my usual announcement about not worrying about baby noise. When we gathered next, at the Bay Area Bookfair, Connie came up to me with a gleam in her eye.

"Remember to make that message again!"

That announcement is always appreciated and it works really well. You can use your own words and put it however you like, but it puts everyone at ease.

Vikki recently told me that while on the "The Community and Resistance Tour" before speaking about prison abolition and incarcerated womens' resistance, she always includes the announcement about being fine with children's noises. But even as she pushes others with this form of activism she admits to me that sometimes children's noises do interrupt her thoughts—after all, that's why we mothers often want childcare. But she works to keep her thoughts together, to look back down at her notes, and get back on track, because, she laughingly states: if a pair of 3 year olds can derail her so easily how does she ever expect to go up against the Prison-Industrial Complex and win? And we play to win, so welcome the sounds of the movement growing.

How to Turn Your Kids into Radicals

by John Chapman

It started as a joke. It was Friday night, which in our family means pizza and movie night. It's the only video time our kids get–we don't watch television, video games, or any of that–just one movie, as a family event. My son, eight years old, was skeptical of the idea of watching Pete's Dragon, which had arrived from Netflix that week. So my partner, mostly as a joke, said, "Well, if you don't want to watch that, you can watch our movie, Food, Inc."

My son stopped. "What's that about?"

We explained that it was a documentary about what is wrong with the food industry, and the bad things that big corporations do to farmers and food.

"That sounds interesting, I want to know what is wrong with our food." His ten-year old sister completely agreed.

So we gathered in the living room and watched it together, both children totally focused on the movie, learning about factory farms, food-borne illnesses, corn-fed vs grass-fed cows, and agribusiness. My son started to lose interest 15 minutes from the end, when the more abstract issues of Genetically Modified Organisms went a little over his eight-year old head—and frankly wasn't the strongest part of the movie. At the end we read off the long list of ways to help change the system and they got up resolving to write their own books about the problems with the food industry. I was really glad that we were eating home-made, vegetarian pizza with nearly all organic ingredients from the food co-op–which spared me the image of two outraged children demanding to know why we would be feeding them corporate food.

The amazing thing is that this was their idea. We didn't particularly encourage them to watch it—we warned them that there might be a lot of sad or gross pictures from the insides of slaughterhouses, and were a little worried that they might not be ready for it. But they wanted to see it—they wanted to know more about what was wrong with the world, and left wanting to do something about it.

Though I have been a progressive for most of my adult life, I haven't been trying to push my politics around my children. Since they were born I haven't been much of an activist. When Seattle's activist community was preparing for the WTO protests, I was preparing for the birth of my first child, and saving vacation to extend paternity leave. I took my daughter to a couple of protests against the Afghanistan war when she was a toddler, riding on my back—but the anger of the protest frightened her, and I didn't want her to grow up thinking that protests were something scary. When my son came along, I found myself pretty well consumed by the day-to-day concerns of raising two children in a healthy and caring way.

We've made clear how we feel about things. They grew up knowing that George Bush was a bad President, and, at an age appropriate level, why. We taught them why we feel war is wrong, why we eat organic food, why we drive a hybrid car and try to use the bus when we can. We talked about racism, pollution, and global warming. We read them books about saving the environment, about people's lives around the world, and the incredible children's books of Patricia Polacco and Dr. Suess—The Lorax and The Butter Battle are still some of the most political kid's books out there. We played them children's music by Dana Lyons.

They have certainly grown up surrounded by progressive values, but we haven't tried to push a lot of politics onto the kids. In part, because their ability to understand some of the more abstract concepts is still growing, but mostly because it feels wrong—pushing political views on a child goes against the grain of any sort of liberatory politics. You can't force people to be radicals; they have to choose that path themselves. All we can do is lay the seeds.

What we have done is to our values: compassion; kindness; fairness; respect. We have tried to teach them that who they are as people matters. We have tried to give them appropriate limits and rules—which kids need—and a safe and healthy space in which to live. We teach them not to hurt others, not to hit, not to tease or put people down, and that nobody should hurt them. And we love them, and listen, which is the most important part of all.

Parenting is an ultimate act of faith and trust. We are entrusted with the life of another human being who is totally dependent on us for everything. We are entrusted to care for that life, to give that human being the love and nurturing they need, and to fill their world with wonder and magic. We are entrusted with helping them grow: first to walk and talk, then to figure out how the world works, how to come into their own as a person, and to eventually go off into that world on their own. And we need to have faith in our own ability to do this incredibly daunting task, in the wonderful people they are, and in the wonderful people they will become. Parenting also means a lot of pain and a lot of tears, from skinned knees to broken hearts, and it's the parents who fall down and fail as much as the kids. In the end, we know that they need to figure out what they believe in for themselves, and we ultimately have no control over that. In the heart of every progressive parent, I think there is a little part that worries, "What will I do if they become Republicans?"

So when an eight and a ten-year-old decide to watch a political documentary because they want to know what is wrong with the world, I feel like maybe, just maybe, I am doing the right thing after all.

Sometimes the most radical things we do are the most everyday and ordinary, and often the most important. Which brings me to a story about my daughter.

A week or two before we watched Food Inc., my daughter brought home a note from a girl in her class, thanking her for standing up for this girl against the teasing of some other classmates. We asked what had happened, and found out that my daughter's three closest friends were among the girls doing the teasing. Which means that my daughter, at ten years old, stood up to her best friends to do what is right. I can remember times in my twenties when I didn't have that kind of courage.

I would love to take credit for that, and say that it was a result of how we raised her. I hope that to some extent it is. But I also know that she has an inner strength and a sense of self that is deeply her own. She has faith in her friends—who really are good kids despite getting caught up in this dynamic.
When a ten-year-old has the courage to stand up for what is right against a playground injustice, it makes me think: that kid will change the world some day. But that sells her short; she is already changing the world, right here and now, and when she and her generation come into their own, this world is going to be in good hands.

Be Good or Be Good At It: a Celebration of Zines, Touring and Community

by Tomas Moniz

I'm not good at a lot of things. I tend to dabble, try something for a minute then move on to the next one. I balk at bureaucracy, at jumping through hopes, at following rules.

Being good is subjective, I admit, but I can say that writing is something I enjoy. And performing, yes, I can say honestly, there's something about it that feels better than drugs—and is healthier too.

And making friends. I like that too.

So whether I am good or not at the aforementioned activities, I've committed to them.

So that's why to celebrate the coming 9th annual San Francisco Zine Fest, I concocted the idea to do a zine tour of northern California.

And why not—zines involve all the things I like to do, that I hope to be good at: writing, drawing, or taking photos. They can involve performance and they are absolutely meaningless without community.

I love zines because I love meeting people. I realized that there are so many people I have met through trading zines, writing letters—and yes, even posting on blog sites—that there could be nothing more grand than to get a bunch of us together in various cities to appreciate one another, to offer praise, to be inspired.

So I put the word out and sure enough two other zines writers Leilani Clark and Dani Burlison of Petals and Bones Zine agreed to set up a whirlwind seven day, six city reading extravaganza.

And the zine world came out to help

We read in a radical infoshop in Santa Cruz, a comic art store in San José, a volunteer run community space in Oakland, an independent bookstore in Davis; we read with a band in Santa Rosa, and finally we ended at the Zine Mecca in the San Francisco's Mission district: Needles and Pens, a store dedicated to zine and DIY culture.

But more than where we read, I gained such a profound appreciation for the power of stories and storytelling. I brought along my daughter to one specific event so she could listen to a story about a Leilani Clark's run in with Bikini Kill, but in the end my daughter asked for two dollars to buy her own copy of Crosshatch's new zine about zombies attacking Oakland.

Kids buying zines: that's a beautiful thing.
So I may never master an art. But I don't have to.

With zines I think I've come to understand the little bit of wisdom given to us by a wonderful Santa Cruz waiter—blond hair aflow down his shoulders, skin tanned from the sun.

His words became the zine tour mantra.

"Be good or be good at." Zines ain't gotta be perfect, they just gotta be.

What's Left (After the first ultrasound—8 weeks)

by Cyrus Armajani

When she says do you see
its little head the beginnings
of arms and legs
I am returned

to an age when I was told
I could see Poseidon's
violin or whatever
it was

I was supposed to see
in the stars. It never made
sense to me. It just seems
like you could point out any group
of stars

or look at the first ultrasound
and say
do you see
Willie Mays
with his back to the infield
or do you see
Lincoln at Ford's Theater or
Dizzy's cheeks or Haymarket Square?
Do you see what's left of Michigan or
Kentucky?
Do you see Vanzetti's mustache?
Sacco's wrist? Do you see Emma
shaking her fist?

So when she says, do you see the heart flutter
fluttering
all I see is
a bear catching Trout.
I see the Mississippi.